Mr. Jawahar K. Kaliani
2504 Crystal Tree Drive
Champaign, IL 61822

D1261035

Physics Lab
in the
Home

SEP   1998

Physics Lab
in the
Home

by BOB FRIEDHOFFER

Illustrated by Joe Hosking

FRANKLIN WATTS
A Division of Grolier Publishing

New York • London • Hong Kong • Sydney
Danbury, Connecticut

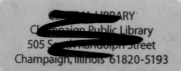
CENTRAL LIBRARY
Champaign Public Library
505 South Randolph Street
Champaign, Illinois 61820-5193

To Timothy White,
A wonderful friend and a great photographer

Interior design and pagination: Carole Desnoes

Library of Congress Cataloging-in-Publication Data

Friedhoffer, Bob.
    Physics lab in the home / by Bob Friedhoffer; illustrated by Joe Hosking.
        p. cm. — (Physical science labs)
    Includes bibliographical references and index.
    Summary: Explores such topics in physics as the properties of water, transmission of heat, evaporation, and air pressure as seen in home plumbing, refrigerators, and other common items.
    ISBN 0-531-11323-X (lib. bdg.)   0-531-15845-4 (pbk.)
    1. Physics—Experiments—Juvenile literature. 2. Physical laboratories—Design and construction—Juvenile literature. [1. Physics—Experiments. 2. Experiments.] I. Hosking, Joe, ill. II. Title. III. Series.
    QC25.F764 1997
    621—dc21   96-36802
                                                      CIP
                                                     AC

©1997 by Bob Friedhoffer
All rights reserved. Published simultaneously in Canada.
Printed in the United States of America.
1 2 3 4 5 6 7 8 9 10 R 06 05 04 03 02 01 00 99 98 97

Acknowledgments

I'd like to thank Annette, for allowing me to "play" scientist, then dragging me away to wonderful and exotic places. Thanks also to Nikki, for a great haircut and lots of fresh new ideas. I'm grateful to J. G. Landels for the information about aqueducts, which I found in *Engineering in the Ancient World*. Finally, I'd like to thank the people who developed word processing programs so I don't have to write in longhand or use a typewriter.

Contents

A Quick Note to Parents and Educators

The other volumes in this series—*Physics Lab in a Supermarket*, *Physics Lab in a Housewares Store*, and *Physics Lab in a Hardware Store*—demonstrate many of the same scientific principles in this book. That has been done with intent. Many of the students who will be attracted to one of these titles may not be attracted to all the others.

Those who are attracted to more than one will have the added pleasure of discovering that a workshop, a kitchen, and a supermarket have many things in common, and that tools and principles used in one might actually be used in the others, too.

Introduction

You might be wondering, "How can there be a science lab at home? Home is home. I eat, sleep, play, and do homework there. A science lab is where scientists hang out, discovering even more things for me to learn in school. Besides, aren't all scientists guys with white coats and long gray beards, who mutter things like: '$E = mc^2$' or 'Ah ha! I've found the secret of living forever!'?"

Well, not exactly! Scientists don't always work in laboratories, don't necessarily wear white coats, and don't talk like they were starring in a sci-fi thriller. There *are* some scientists with long gray beards— usually they are older men.

Almost anyone can make scientific observations and do experiments, even kids. And anywhere that you make observations and perform experiments can be considered a science laboratory. Entomologists, scientists who study insects, do most of their work in forests, jungles, and backyards. Herpetologists, scientists who study reptiles such as snakes and lizards, hunt for their subjects where they live—in wooded areas, swamps, and fields.

Some astronomers, scientists who study planets, stars, galaxies, and everything else in the cosmos, set up telescopes in their backyards, in parks, or on mountaintops. These scientists study in "field laboratories," and so can you. Your home can be your field laboratory.

Did you ever wonder how certain things in your home worked? When I was a youngster (lots of years ago when the only good music was rock and roll, long before walkman-type tape players and CDs), I always wanted to know what made things work—things like light switches, refrigerators, dishwashers, washing machines, toilets, sinks, freezers, door locks, hinges, vacuum cleaners, coffee makers, juicers, windows, and plumbing pipes.

After disassembling (the easy part) and reassembling (the harder part) lots of household "stuff," I learned that even the most complex of these items worked on some very basic principles. All of them worked (when I was able to put them back together properly) because of science and applied science, which is called technology. Once I looked at the simple components that make these items work, they were easy—or at least easier— to understand. This book will show you how to perform experiments and observations at home and help you figure out where and how science is used in your home.

Scattered throughout these chapters you will find a safety symbol. Ask an adult to help you wherever you see this symbol. The symbol indicates that the experiment is a little bit dangerous or difficult. I'd hate to see you get discouraged or hurt while you are learning about science in your home. Throughout the book you'll also find words in *italic* type. These words are defined in the glossary at the back of the book.

There are three other books in this series that explain how you can conduct scientific observations and experiments with material found in hardware stores, housewares stores, and supermarkets. If you like this book and think your friends, parents, and teachers would like it, the author's name is Bob Friedhoffer. Go to the library and check out the books, or even better, go to the bookstore and buy them. If you don't like this book . . . don't tell anyone.

CHAPTER ONE

Plumbing

WHY IS IT CALLED PLUMBING?

The word "plumbing" comes from the Latin word for lead, as in "a lead pipe" or "a lead fishing weight." The chemical symbol for lead is "Pb."

What's the connection? Plumbing pipes were originally made of lead, a soft, easily worked metal. The ancient Romans used lead to make plumbing pipes, kitchen utensils, jewelry, and other items. Some historians believe that Roman civilization fell into disarray because the population was suffering from lead poisoning. The lead from their pipes and utensils could have been transferred into the Romans' food and water. When they ate and drank, the lead may have entered their bodies, causing brain damage and death.

How did the Romans get water from the mountains—where it was found in lakes, rivers, and streams—to the cities where it was used for cooking, drinking, washing, and bathing? Did they carry it in buckets? Haul it in tanker cars? Use pumps?

The answer to each question is no. Instead, they constructed long channels from the mountains to the cities. These channels were the famous Roman aqueducts. "Aque" comes from the Latin word for water, and "duct" comes from the Latin word meaning "to lead" (as in "You can lead a horse to water, but you can't make him take a bath"). Pumps were not necessary. Why? Let's take a short side trip and find out.

IS THE SURFACE OF A LAKE OR OCEAN REALLY FLAT?

Did you ever see a body of water—a lake or pond or pool—where all the water was piled up on one side and there was no water on the other side? Chances are, unless you're from an alternate universe, you haven't. (Waves that slowly settle down or a stack of piled up ice don't count.)

Most of the water on our planet—in rivers, oceans, or lakes—is a *liquid*. (You can find out more about liquids and other states of *matter* in the Appendix at the back of this book.) If you look across the surface of a body of water, it looks relatively flat. Observation 1 lets you see this for yourself.

OBSERVATION 1

Fill a cereal bowl or soup bowl with water. Put the bowl in the kitchen sink. Tilt the bowl up to one side, and then lay it flat on its bottom.

Some of the water should have spilled out when you tilted the bowl. What happened when you laid the bowl flat again? When the water stopped sloshing around, how did the surface of the water look? Do you think that the water's surface is really flat?

If you could fly straight up in the air near the edge of the ocean, you would eventually reach a height where you would see that the surface of the water is actually curved, not flat. The reason is that Earth itself is curved like a ball. Because *gravity* pulls everything on Earth's surface, including water, toward Earth's center, the surface of a body of water is curved, too.

So why does the surface of a lake or ocean look flat? Because Earth is so large—its circumference is about 24,000 miles (40,000 km). The curve of Earth's surface is so gradual that we cannot see it from ground level.

Imagine that you are in a hot-air balloon at the seashore. As the balloon rises into the air, your point of view begins to change. The higher you go, the more ocean you can see. If you could rise high enough, you would eventually be able to see the curve of Earth. If you went even higher, you would see that our planet is really a huge ball. The only way you could get far enough above Earth to see it as a ball would be by riding in a spacecraft powered by a rocket. But, Observation 2 will let you experience this effect without ever leaving the ground.

OBSERVATION 2

Close one eye. Hold a basketball about 6 inches (15 cm) away from your open eye, and look at the center of the ball. Note that just by looking, you really can't tell if the ball is spherical (ball-shaped) or flat. If you move the ball away from your eye slowly, the ball will begin to look curved. When you move the ball far enough away from your eye, it takes on the shape of a circle or sphere.

BACK TO THE AQUEDUCTS

The ancient Romans were impressive engineers. Vitruvius was a well-respected Roman architect who lived from about 70 B.C. to 25 B.C. His books, which are still studied today, point out that water seeks its own level, in both closed systems (pipes) and open systems—like the water in the bowl you observed.

One problem in building a closed system was that technology in Roman times was inadequate. The only materials available for pipes were lead or earthenware pottery, but both were costly and unreliable. Vitruvius preferred pottery for the pipes because he suspected that lead was dangerous. He also felt that an open system, such as an aqueduct was better because it was easier to repair than a closed system.

As we mentioned earlier, the Roman engineers figured out that the best way to get water to the cities over valleys, without using a closed pipe system, was to build aqueducts—stone bridges with channels on top to carry the water. The channels could be lined with mortar or cement to prevent the water from leaking through cracks. Some were up to 35 miles (56 km) long. These engineering marvels can be seen in places such as Segovia, Spain and Nimes, France.

Vitruvius knew that the "drop"—the distance that the water fell—did not have to be very large to keep the water flowing. It could be as little as 1 inch (2.5 cm) for every 41 feet (12.5 m) in length. How is this possible? Because water seeks its own level.

But, enough about the ancient Romans. Now, let's jump forward in time. In the not-too-distant past, lead was used in our water pipes, too. It was cheap and easy to work. Lead was also being used in gasoline, paint, and many other materials.

Gasoline manufacturers started adding lead tetra-ethyl to automobile gasoline in the 1920s to improve engine performance. Later, nutritional scientists found that crops grown near busy highways contained larger proportions of lead than crops grown elsewhere.

In the 1970s, when it became common knowledge that lead

was toxic, this additive was banned for use in new cars. Engines were designed that could run on gasoline without the added lead. As a result, leaded gasoline was banned, and the lead content of crops has been greatly reduced. About the same time, people stopped using lead water pipes. Now, water pipes are made of copper or plastic, or even concrete if they are very large.

GOING WITH THE FLOW

If you live in a large city such as New York, Los Angeles, or Chicago, you might have noticed big wooden water tanks on top of some apartment or office buildings. If you live in a smaller city or town, you might see a different type of water-storage tank—a water tower—in the center of town. Both kinds of tanks accomplish the same purpose. A tank on top of a building supplies that building with water. Tanks in the middle of town supply water to the whole town, except of course the people who have their own wells.

Roman aqueducts delivered water with the aid of gravity, so pumps were not used. The water tanks in our towns and cities today generally need pumps to get the water to the top of the tanks, and then rely on the principle that a liquid in a "closed system" will seek its own level. This is what causes water to flow down the pipes and into everyone's faucets.

EXPERIMENT 1

Materials
A 3-foot (1-m) length of clear, flexible, plastic tubing with
    a 3/8-inch (1-cm) diameter
A kitchen funnel
A pitcher of water

Procedure
CAUTION: Perform this experiment in a sink.
1. Place the funnel in one end of the plastic tube, and add water until the tube is half full.

2. Hold both ends of the tube at the same height above the sink. Be sure not to block the opening at either end of the tube. Is the water level on both sides of the tube the same distance above the sink?
3. Slowly raise one end of the tube while holding the other end steady. Wait a moment to let the water settle down. What happens to the water level on both sides of the tube?

Results

The water level stays the same on both sides of the tube because water seeks its own level in a closed system.

For the same reason, as long as a water outlet is lower than the level of water in a storage tank, the water will continue to flow—even if the outlet is higher than the point where the water pipe enters the building. If the Romans had built closed water systems like ours, they could have laid pipes that ran up and down hills and across valleys. As long as the water source was higher than the point where the water eventually came out, the water would have flowed "uphill" in between.

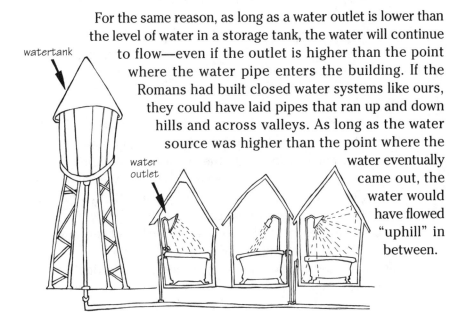

watertank

water outlet

EXPERIMENT 2

Materials

Two empty plastic soda bottles
Four tags or a roll of masking tape
A marking pen
Two 3-foot (1-m) lengths of clear, flexible plastic tubing with
a 3/8-inch (1-cm) diameter
Silicone sealing glue
A knife to cut the bottles and tubing
A kitchen funnel
A pitcher of water

Procedure

CAUTION: This experiment should be attempted only with the supervision of an adult. It should be done over a kitchen sink. Be careful when using sharp objects to prepare the materials.

1. Using the marking pen, write the letters "A" and "B" on two tags or pieces of masking tape. Attach one label to each soda bottle. Write the letters "C" and "D" on the remaining tags or two additional pieces of masking tape, and attach one label to each piece of tubing.

2. Using the drawing on the opposite page as a guide, cut one slit in the shape of an "X" close to the bottom of Bottle A.

3. Cut two X-shaped slits close to the bottom of Bottle B. The "X's" should be on opposite sides of the bottle.

4. Insert one end of Tube C into the "X" of Bottle A. When you do this, the "X" will become a hole. Use the silicone glue to hold the tubing in place. (Be sure that you don't block the center of the tube with glue.)

5. Insert the other end of Tube C into Bottle B and apply glue to hold the tubing in place.

6. Insert one end of Tube D into the other "X" in Bottle B and glue it in place.

7. After the glue has dried, fill both bottles with water to see that they don't leak, and then empty the bottles.

8. Place the funnel into the top of Bottle A, and add water to Bottle A until it is half full. Note what happens to the water.

9. Lift Bottle A, and watch what happens to the water in Tube D.

Results

The water should flow through Tube C, into Bottle B, and then into Tube D. When you lift Bottle A, you will see how water can run uphill in a closed system. As long as Bottle A is higher than the top of Tube D, water should flow out of Tube D.

CHAPTER TWO

Faucets and Pipes

We now know how water gets into our homes, but how do we keep it from flooding us out? We use faucets. A faucet is a type of valve that we can control to make water flow or stop flowing. We don't know exactly when the first water faucet was invented, but we do know that a type of faucet was used in Greece more than 2,000 years ago.

RUBBER WASHERS

Rubber washers are used in plumbing because they form water-tight seals at faucet connections and other joints. They can be made from either artificial or natural rubber, and they are usually elastic. When an elastic object is deformed (twisted, bent, or pulled out of shape), it will return, or try to return, to its original shape. As the rubber washer tries to return to its original shape, it blocks any loose joints or connections that might otherwise allow water to pass.

A good example of this can be seen in a gar-

handle

rubber washer

garden hose

den hose connected to an outside faucet. The coupling of the hose and faucet has to be loose enough to be tightened by hand, but tight enough so that water doesn't leak. The illustration on the previous page shows how a rubber washer blocks potential leaks when it is squished down in all the proper places.

HOW DO FAUCETS WORK?

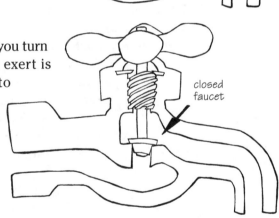

As you probably know, a faucet usually has a handle at the top. When the handle is twisted one way, water flows out. When the handle is twisted in the opposite direction, water stops flowing.

open faucet

When you twist the handle of a typical faucet, you are operating a type of simple machine called a *first-class lever*. As you turn the handle, the force you exert is multiplied, enabling you to easily turn the screw— another type of simple machine—found inside the faucet. (You can learn much more about levers, screws, and other simple tools in the Appendix at the back of this book.)

closed faucet

If the faucet handle did not function as a lever, you would probably not be able turn the faucet on and off. If you tried to turn the screw itself with your fingers, you would find it almost impossible because the water in the pipe is under a great deal of *pressure* and because the screw's movement is affected by *friction*.

As you turn the handle, the screw moves up and down inside the faucet. Below the screw is a rubber washer that seals the two chambers of the faucet from each other. If this seal is broken, the faucet may begin to leak.

To repair a leaky faucet, you usually have to replace the rubber washer. These washers come in many different types and sizes. Hardware stores—or hardware departments of large stores like Walmart™—usually sell small packages of washers of various sizes. One of these washers should fit your faucet.

PROJECT 1

Materials
An adjustable (monkey or Crescent®) wrench
A screwdriver
A soft towel or sponge

Procedure
CAUTION: Do not attempt to replace or repair a faucet without an adult's supervision! If you make a mistake, you and everything around you will get very wet. If you're trying to replace a washer in a hot-water faucet, be careful not to not burn yourself with the water or the hot pipe.

1. ***Turn off the faucet's water supply.*** If you don't turn it off, you will probably flood the house. You can shut off the water supply by turning two handles (usually found under the sink) on the pipes that run into the sink. Once you think the main water supply has been shut off, find out by turning the faucet on. If water comes out, there is a problem. Go back under the sink and try again. When you're sure that you've shut off the water supply, you're ready to disassemble the faucet.

2. Loosen the screw that holds the handle of the faucet in place. Put the screw and the handle in a safe place, away from the drain. (That way you won't drop the screw down the drain like I did.)
3. Carefully fit the wrench (another lever) around the large nut at the base of the handle. If the nut is shiny chrome or brass, you may want to cushion the jaws of the wrench with the soft towel. This will keep the polished finish from getting scratched.
4. When the nut is loose, continue to twist it off with your fingers. Put the nut in a safe place along with the handle and the screw.
5. Now you must take apart the faucet-screw mechanism. It can probably be extracted with the aid of the adjustable wrench.
6. When you have taken apart the mechanism and removed it, examine the bottom. You should see a rubber washer—it is usually black or red. (Note which side of the washer is up and which side is down.)
7. In the center of the rubber washer on the faucet-screw mechanism you will find a small screw that holds the washer in place. Remove this screw and the old washer.
8. Choose a new washer that matches the size of the old washer, and put the new one in. Once the new washer is properly positioned, replace the screw that holds it.
9. Replace the faucet-screw mechanism, the nut that holds it in place, the handle, and the screw. Make sure that everything has been properly tightened.
10. Turn the faucet handle to the "off" position.
11. Go back under the sink and turn on the water supply. If water is not spraying out of the top of the faucet, you have put everything back together properly. If water is not dripping from the faucet, you have successfully replaced the old washer. Turn the faucet on and off a few times to seat the washer. If all goes well, you can tell your folks that you just saved them a $50 or $60 plumbing bill.

CHAPTER THREE

Water Seeks Its Own Level (On the Way Out)

As you've seen, the water from a water tower can run down a pipe, travel underground, and then flow up again when it reaches your house—even if it eventually comes out of a faucet on an upper floor. This ability of water to flow uphill and downhill in a closed pipe also makes it easier for water to leave your home.

THE TRAP

First, we'll visit the kitchen sink. If you can get under the sink and move some of the cleaning supplies, paper bags, and other stuff your folks store there, you will see the pipe that runs out from the sink's drain. It's bent like an "S" that's lying on its side. The lowest part of the pipe is called the trap. As water from the sink flows into the top of the pipe, the water in the trap

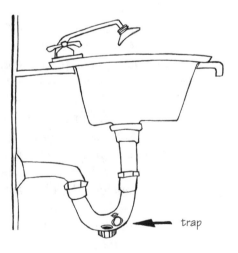

trap

seeks its own level. As a result, it starts to flow out of the trap toward the sewer line, pulled by gravity. When all the water drains out of the sink, the water continues running through the trap until the water level is equal on both sides.

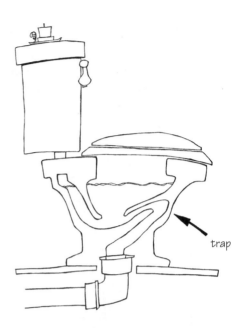

trap

A trap serves two purposes. First of all, it prevents foul smells from the sewer from entering the house. Those smells are blocked by the water in the pipe. Secondly, a large cap screwed into the bottom of most traps allows access to the inside of the pipe. This lets us clean out the pipe if it gets filled with dirt or grease. It also allows us to retrieve anything that falls into the drain, such as a ring or other small object.

You'll find a similar trap in the bathroom, built into the pipe that leaves the bathtub. There's also a trap built into the porcelain of the toilet bowl, but do not try to examine it. There may be all sorts of germs lurking about, waiting to pounce on you and make you ill. Like those in the other drains, this water-filled trap keeps odors from the sewer out of the house.

EXPERIMENT 3

Materials
A 3-foot (1-m) length of clear, flexible plastic tubing with a
    3/8-inch (1-cm) diameter
A kitchen funnel
A pitcher of water
A friend

Procedure
CAUTION: Be sure to do this over the kitchen sink.

1. Bend the tube into an "S" shape and ask your friend to hold the tube in that shape.

2. Place the funnel in one end of the tube and slowly pour water into the funnel. As you pour the water in, notice how it flows through the tube.
3. Keep pouring water until it starts flowing out the other end. When you stop pouring, examine what happend to the water in the "S" curve.

Results
You should see that part of the curve stays full of water, even when the water stops flowing. The water level on both sides of the lower curve of the "S" stays the same because —TAH DAH!—water seeks its own level. The trap under a sink, tub, or toilet works in the same way. So now we've seen how water enters and leaves the house. All of this, because water seeks its own level in a closed system. Science can be so cool!

CLEANING OUT
BLOCKED SEWER LINES

How do drains get clogged? Sometimes materials like paper, food particles, oils, grease, or hair go down the drain and block the flow of water. This material can be cleaned out in a number of ways.

Some people use chemicals that react with the blocked material, making it liquid enough to be washed away with water. Other people use a *plunger*. A plunger is a rubber hemisphere (half-ball) or cup attached to a wooden handle. Generally, plungers are used to unclog toilet bowls, but they should not be used by the fainthearted. When it is necessary to use one, conditions in the toilet are probably pretty nasty. Maybe you should keep a pair of nose clips with the plunger, just in case.

To clear a drain, place the bottom of the plunger in the accumulated water above the drain. The rubber should be in contact with the porcelain so that air gets trapped inside the cup. When the handle is pushed down vigorously, the rubber of the cup collapses, decreasing the volume within the cup, and forcefully injecting the air and water that were inside the cup into the drain. This action may have to be repeated three or four times. Hopefully, the combination of air and water is enough to clear the blockage.

If the plunger doesn't work, you might have to call in a plumber to use a snake. A plumber's snake is basically a long flexible wire that mechanically pushes the blockage out through the length of the pipe.

CHAPTER FOUR

Surface Tension

Water has other properties we can explore with materials found around the house. Have you ever wondered why water, if it's not being disturbed in some way, settles down into a nice smooth surface? This is the result of an interesting phenomenon called *surface tension*.

Water molecules are drawn to each other because of a force called *cohesion*. The water molecules below the surface of a body of water are all attracted equally to each other. Those on the surface of the water are pulled downward by the molecules underneath, and sideways by the water molecules around them. This results in a "skin" of water being formed on top. This skin is called surface tension. Certain water bugs take advantage of surface tension by gliding across the water's surface, without breaking through and falling into the water.

EXPERIMENT 4

Materials
A bowl of water
Black pepper
A drop of liquid soap

Procedure
1. Fill the bowl with water and sprinkle some black pepper on the surface of the water.

2. Wash your hands and dry them well.
3. Touch the tip of your index finger to the surface of the water-pepper mixture. What happens?
4. Put a drop of liquid soap on your fingertip and touch the drop of soap to the surface of the water–pepper mixture. What happens?

Results

When you touched the finger without the soap to the water, not much happened. Perhaps a small circle of clear water appeared around your finger. When you touched the soap drop to the water though, the pepper rapidly scattered to the sides of the bowl. This is because the soap decreased the surface tension of the water in the center of the bowl. When the surface tension in the middle of the bowl decreased, the pepper was pulled to the edge of the bowl where the surface tension—the cohesion of the water molecules—was stronger.

CHAPTER FIVE

Hot and Cold

What does it mean when people say that it's cold? There are several answers to this question. Different people are affected by the same temperature in different ways. Have you ever been out with a friend who said that it was too cold, while you thought it was perfect or even too hot? Or maybe the opposite happened—you thought it was too cold and your friend thought it was too hot. The following experiment shows that how we perceive temperature depends on a variety of factors.

EXPERIMENT 5

Materials
Three identical, deep mixing bowls
Hot water (but not burning hot)
Warm water
Cold water
A friend
A handkerchief to be used as a blindfold

Procedure
1. Fill one bowl with cold water, the second bowl with warm water, and the remaining bowl with hot water.
2. Cover your friend's eyes with the blindfold.
3. Place your friend's hand in the bowl of cold water and ask if it feels hot, warm, or cold.
4. Put the same hand in the bowl of hot water and ask

your friend which bowl she thinks it is—hot, warm, or cold.
5. Do the same with the warm water.

Results
Repeat this experiment several times and you will find that your friend answers incorrectly more than once. Our sense of touch is not absolutely accurate. It can be fooled when comparing temperatures.

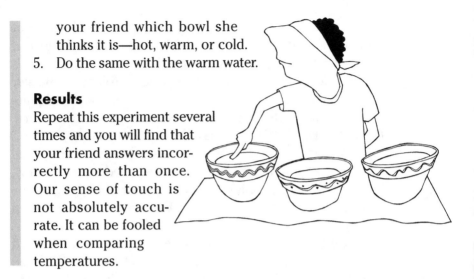

WHAT IS HEAT?

In the summer we cool our homes, and in the winter we heat them. We keep our refrigerators going to keep our food cold. What *is* heat? Think about that—and think about this joke:

A mother talking to her son: "Put your sweater on. It's cold outside"
Son's reply: "And if I put my sweater on, will it be warm outside?"

What does "cold" mean? It is the absence of heat. That probably sounds like a wise-guy answer, but it's not. The next question has to be, "So what *is* heat?"

In 1669, a German chemist named Johann Joachim Becher stated that combustible (burnable) materials contained phlogiston, an invisible fluid that allowed the materials to burn. *Phlogiston* (FLOW-JIST-ON) was a Greek word meaning "burned." Wood was made up of wood ashes and phlogiston, theorized Georg Ernst Stahl, a German scientist who lived from 1660–1734. Later, the theory of phlogiston was shown to be false by the famous French scientist Antoine Lavoisier, who lived from 1743–1794.

During the 1700s, scientists believed that heat was caused by a weightless, invisible fluid known as "caloric." When an object was warm, it contained caloric. This fluid was thought to pass from warm objects to cold ones. If you placed your cold hands on a warm stove, caloric moved from the stove to your hands.

British physicist Benjamin Thompson, who lived from 1753–1814 and was also known as Count Rumford, was the first person on record to realize that heat is actually connected to motion. At that time, he was overseeing the boring of cannons for the British army. Until then, everyone believed that heat from the boring process was a release of caloric. Count Rumford analyzed what was happening and discovered that the mechanical action of boring caused the heat.

Today, we believe that heat is connected to the motion of molecules. The faster the molecules move, the more energy they have and the greater the heat created. By the way, we can't see these movements. For example, the molecules in your desk are moving all the time—sort of marching in place. They move because they have absorbed heat energy from the surrounding air.

Heat can be measured using any one of three temperature scales—the Fahrenheit scale, the Celsius or Centigrade scale, and the Kelvin or Absolute scale. According to the Fahrenheit scale, water freezes at 32°F and boils at 212° F.* According to the Celsius scale, water freezes at 0°C and boils at 100°C. According to the Kelvin scale, water freezes at 273 K and boils at 373 K. (Note that the degree symbol is not used with the Kelvin scale.) There can be no temperature colder than 0 K or absolute zero. Molecules don't move at all at that temperature.

HEAT ON THE MOVE

You've probably noticed that heat can move around. If you turn on a radiator, it gets hot, and so does the room, and so, eventually, do you. But how does that heat move? Heat is transferred in three ways: *conduction, radiation*, and *convection*.

Conduction

Conduction occurs when something warm is in contact with something cooler. The heat flows from the warmer object to the cooler one. For instance, when you are holding a cold glass of soda, the heat from your hand travels into the glass. Your hand feels cold because heat is being taken away by the glass of soda. If you held the glass long enough, the temperature of the soda glass would be the same as the temperature of your hand.

Some materials conduct heat well. These materials can be called *conduc-*

---

*The boiling point of water may vary depending on altitude. To learn more about how air pressure influences boiling point, go to the Appendix.

tors. Usually, metals are excellent conductors. Some materials conduct heat quite poorly. In general, objects with lots of air pockets like towels and pot holders are poor conductors. These are called *insulators*.

OBSERVATION 3

Fill an ice cream cone with your favorite flavor and hold it in your hand.

Does it feel cold? Probably not. It doesn't feel cold because the cone acts as an insulator. That means that the material the cone is made from—usually wheat flour —is not a good conductor of heat. The heat of your hand is not being transferred at a rate you notice to the ice cream inside the cone.

Now for the hard part! (Just remember that you're doing this to advance your knowledge of science.) Lick the ice cream. Besides the taste of the ice cream, what else do you notice as you eat the ice cream? You should notice that the ice cream feels cold.

Your tongue, being warmer than the ice cream, has transferred some of its heat to the ice cream. As a result, the ice cream changes its state from a *solid* to a liquid. (The Three states of matter— solid, liquid, and gas—are discussed in more detail in the Appendix at the back of this book.)

This observation proves that science can be a lot of fun, and tasty too!

Radiation

Heat can be transferred by *radiation*. (This use of the word "radiation" has little to do with nuclear radiation or atomic bombs.) If you are sitting around a fire on a cool night you will

notice that the side of your body nearest the fire is warmer than the side of your body away from the fire. This is not because the fire heats the air and the air in turn heats you. If this were true, your whole body would be heated equally.

The light given off by the fire is part of the *electromagnetic spectrum*. Some light in this spectrum is visible, other light is invisible. All visible light, including light from the fire, contains heat energy. It is the heat energy from the firelight that is heating the side of your body closest to the fire.

English scientist Sir Isaac Newton, who lived from 1642 to 1727, was the first person to understand the visible light portion of the electromagnetic spectrum. He discovered that white light, such as sunlight, is composed of seven colors. When he

placed a prism in the path of a beam of sunlight, the prism broke the light into the colors of the rainbow: red, orange, yellow, green, blue, indigo, and violet. (To memorize the colors of the rainbow or spectrum, remember the name "Roy G. Biv." Each letter of that name stands for a color of the spectrum in the proper order.)

Newton also passed the individual colors of the spectrum through additional prisms. He found that they could not be broken down any further. He also recombined the seven individual colors to form white light. Newton published his results in 1704 in an important scientific book called *Opticks*.

In 1800, British astronomer Sir William Herschel measured the temperature of the various colors of the spectrum. He found that red light had the highest temperature and violet light had the lowest temperature. He then discovered that if he measured the temperature of the space directly above red light, the temperature went higher, even though there was nothing to be seen. He didn't know it, but he had discovered light that is invisible to the human eye—infrared light.

(Besides his ground-breaking work in the field of optics, Newton also proposed the three laws of motion and invented an important field of mathematics called calculus. For hundreds of years, the British government has valued scientific inquiry and recognized the accomplishments of scientists. Outstanding scientists such as Newton, and Herschel, were knighted. That's why they have a "Sir" in front of their names.)

Another time you might notice heat radiation is on a cool but sunny day. If you stay in the shadow of a large tree or a building you will probably be a lot chillier than if you stand in direct sunlight, where you are warmed by radiant energy from the sun.

Think about this. The sun is shining at the center of the solar system. The space between Earth and the sun is pretty much empty except for the planets Venus and Mercury and some occasional space dust. There is no air or other *gases* to transfer heat. So the sun's rays shine through space and heat up our planet, and anything on its surface, by radiation.

The sun also gives off energy from the UV or ultraviolet (beyond violet) portion of the electromagnetic spectrum. UV light allows people hanging out on the beach to get suntans. Like infrared rays, UV rays are invisible to the naked eye.

UV can be helpful. It can be used to kill bacteria in water or to "set" certain synthetic glues and plastics.

But these ultraviolet rays can also be dangerous. They can cause sunburns, and even cancer. Most UV is filtered out by the ozone layer high in the stratosphere. That is why many people are concerned about the "hole" in the ozone layer. Without enough ozone, humans and most other living things could be subjected to massive doses of UV.

Some people say that the answer is to wear more sunscreen and thicker clothing. But this does not appear to be a satisfactory answer for people or animals who spend much of their time outdoors when the sun is high in the sky. Plants too can be damaged by excess doses of UV, and they can't come inside.

EXPERIMENT 6

Materials
Two identical paper cups
Black paint
A paint brush

Two identical thermometers
A sunny day

Procedure
1. Paint the outside edges and the bottom of the cups black and let them dry for several hours.
2. Punch a small hole in the bottom of each cup and turn each cup upside down.
3. Place a thermometer inside each cup through the hole in the bottom.
4. Place both cups on the floor or ground near each other—one in the sun, one in the shade. Make sure that each cup's environment is the same, except for the sunlight. One should not be closer to a heating vent, radiator, air conditioner, or puddle of water than the other.

Results
You should find that the radiant energy of the sun caused the cup in the sun to become warmer than the cup in the shade.

Convection

Convection is the transfer of heat by the movement of fluids. A fluid is anything that flows, so when we talk of heat transfer by convection we are concerned with liquids and gases.

Convection occurs when a fluid warms up. When a fluid is heated, its molecules absorb heat, start to move faster, and the space between the molecules increases. In other words, the fluid expands. As a result, the fluid near the heat source becomes less dense and begins to rise. Cooler fluid moves into the area where the warm fluid used to be. As that cooler fluid is heated, it too moves upward. This cycle continues until the heat source is removed or equilibrium (a balance) is reached. This process occurs inside an oven, a boiling pot of water, and a campfire.

An ordinary lightbulb in your house shows convection at work. How? The air directly above and around the lightbulb is heated. As it heats up, it becomes less dense. Being less dense, it starts to rise. As it rises, the cooler air in the room rushes in and takes the warm air's place. When that air warms up, it begins to rise and the cycle continues until the light is turned off. Of course, you can't see the air that's getting warmed, but you can show that it's there.

EXPERIMENT 7

Materials
A 36-inch (90-cm) wooden stick (a yardstick)
String
An electric drill and bit
Two identical, small brown paper bags
A short table lamp minus its shade
A nail
A hammer
A doorway with an electrical outlet nearby

Procedure
CAUTION: This experiment should only be done with adult supervision. Make sure that the hot lightbulb doesn't burn anyone or any-thing. Try to do this experiment in a place with a tile or cement floor such as a bathroom or garage. Ask permission before putting a nail in the doorframe.
1. Drill a small hole in the center of the wooden stick.
2. Cut a 24-inch (60-cm) length of string and push it through the hole in the stick. Knot the end of the string

several times, so that it cannot be pulled back through the hole.

3. Hold the other end of the string and make sure that the stick is level when it hangs.
4. Using the nail, punch a hole in the center of the bottom of each bag.
5. Cut two 12-inch (30-cm) pieces of string and thread each one through the hole in one of the paper bags. Knot the end of the string several times, so that it cannot be pulled back through the hole.

6. Using the hammer, pound the nail into a wooden door-frame (at the top, close to the center). Tie the string attached to the wooden stick to the nail. The stick should be hanging level.
7. Tie one bag close to each end of the stick (open end downward). See the illustration above. Adjust each bag's distance from the end of the stick until the stick is once again hanging level.
8. Place the lamp on the floor, directly under one of the bags, turn it on, and watch what happens.

Results

A few moments after you light the bulb, the air above the lamp begins to heat up and the bag above the lamp starts to rise. Why does the bag rise? As the air is heated, its molecules speed up and move farther apart, so its density decreases. Then, the cooler, denser air surrounding the lamp moves in and forces the warmer air upward. The warmer air eventually enters the bag, displacing some of the cooler air inside. Because the air inside the bag is now less dense (lighter), the surrounding air pushes the bag upward.

In other words, the lightbulb created a convection current, which transferred heat by air—a fluid, and the bag rose. As the warm air rose, cooler air took its place, warmed up, and rose in turn.

DRYING CLOTHES

"Science involved with drying your clothes? Harrumph! Sounds like a lot of baloney to me. All you do is put the wet clothes on a clothesline or in a dryer and they dry. It's that simple."

Most people, if asked whether science is used in drying clothes, would probably say something like the above. But if it weren't for scientific principles and the use of heat, we'd be walking around in clothes that are sopping wet.

When clothes are washed, either by machine or by hand, they are usually wrung or spun to get rid of a lot of the water they've absorbed. If the excess water was not forced out by one of these methods, the clothes would take much longer to dry. Wringing the clothes is similar to squeezing out a wet sponge. When the sponge or the fibers of clothing are squeezed, much of the water is forced out.

OBSERVATION 4

CAUTION: Do this over a sink or wash basin.
You will need a "bone-dry" sponge—that means completely dry! Turn on the water, and soak the sponge thoroughly. What happens as the sponge gets wet? It expands.

Once the sponge is soaked, squeeze it until it's as dry as you can get it. Why do you think the water runs out?

When a sponge—or clothing—absorbs water, the water must go somewhere. The fibers of the material

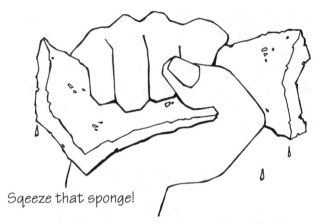

Sqeeze that sponge!

expand and are held in place through capillary action. What does this mean exactly? When you wring out a sponge or an item of clothing, the fibers are squeezed together and the capillaries—the little tubes or spaces where the water is held—are forced together and can no longer hold water.

After clothes are washed, they may be hung on a clothesline to dry. The clothesline can be in a backyard, in a basement, or, if you live in an apartment building, it may

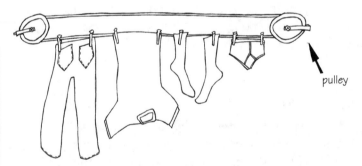

pulley

be right outside your window. Since you can't stand below a clothesline outside your window, there has to be a way to get the clothes from one end of the line to the other without stretching out too far or climbing a really tall ladder, so a pulley is used. (The pulley—a type of simple machine—is discussed in the Appendix.)

Clothes dry in a couple of different ways. Some of the water drips off and falls to the ground. The water that doesn't drip off is held in place by the fibers of the clothing. So how does that water leave the clothing? It *evaporates* or turns into a gas, but the air around the clothing has to be dry so that the water can evaporate. A warm, sunny day is best for drying clothes; the heat of the sun makes the water evaporate faster.

THE CLOTHES DRYER

The clothes dryer was designed as a device to aid the harried housekeeper. Instead of being hung on a clothesline, the clothes are put into this mechanical marvel and come out dry, ready to

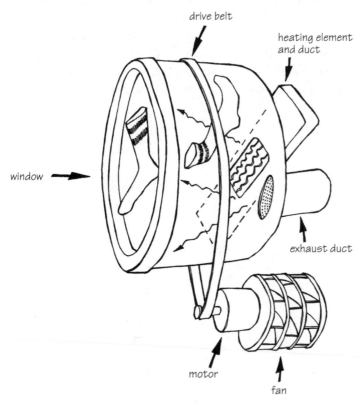

drive belt

heating element and duct

window

exhaust duct

motor

fan

be folded. The clothes dryer eliminates the need to hang up wet articles, one by one, and then take them down when they are dry. It also makes life easier when the weather is inclement (crummy).

The dryer is basically a rotating, perforated cylinder with a box built around it. Heated air is forced through the cylinder and quickly evaporates the water held in the clothing's fibers. The heated air, now laden with moisture, is vented outside the dryer, and usually outside the building through an exhaust duct. The air is usually heated in one of two ways—by fire from gas or oil, or by electricity.

Before clothes are placed in a dryer they are usually wrung out, so that less water will have to be evaporated. This can be done manually, by squeezing or twisting the clothes with your hands, by a mangler, or by the spin cycle in a washing machine.

A mangler consists of two rubber rollers that are turned by a crank. The soaking wet clothes are run between the rollers and the water is mechanically squeezed out. In a spin cycle, the basket in the washer spins, and the water is forced out of the basket and the clothing by *rotational inertia*, which many people call *centrifugal force*. This is a force caused by rotation that moves things outward, away from the center of rotation.

CHAPTER SIX

The Refrigerator

WHY DO WE NEED REFRIGERATORS?

We refrigerate foods at home to inhibit or retard the growth of bacteria. Most harmful bacteria grow more slowly at temperatures lower than 40°F (4°C) than at room temperature. (And most harmful bacteria in the home are destroyed at temperatures greater than 160°F [70°C].)

EXPERIMENT 8

Materials
Three identical glass jars with screw-on lids
Paper towels
Masking tape
A marking pen
Milk
A measuring cup
A saucepan, half full of cold water
A thermometer that measures up to 212°F (100°C)
A potholder or kitchen towel

Procedure
CAUTION: Before attempting this experiment, get your parents' approval. Be careful not to burn yourself. Also, make sure that your folks don't accidentally throw out part of your experiment.

1. Clean each jar and lid thoroughly with soap and water.
2. Rinse each jar so that no soap remains, and dry each jar with a clean paper towel.
3. Using masking tape and the marking pen, label the lids 1, 2, and 3.
4. Partially fill each jar with milk. Use a measuring cup to make sure that each jar contains the same amount of milk.
5. Screw the lids on Jars 1 and 2.
6. Put Jar 1 in the refrigerator and Jar 2 in a warm place— maybe next to the refrigerator. (This jar will act as the experimental *control*.) Place Jar 3 (without its lid) in the saucepan containing water. Then, put the thermometer into Jar 3.
7. Slowly bring the water to a boil. Once the thermometer in the milk has maintained a temperature of 160°F (70°C) for at least 2 minutes, remove the pan from the stove.
8. Remove the thermometer from the jar, taking care not to burn yourself.

9. Using a pot holder or kitchen towel, remove Jar 3 from the hot water and screw on the lid. Place Jar 3 next to Jar 2.
10. After all three jars have sat for 3 or 4 days, open each jar and sniff the contents.

Results

The milk in Jar 2, the control, should smell sour because bacteria caused a chemical reaction in the milk. The milk in Jar 1 should smell fresh because very little bacterial growth takes place in a cool environment, such as the refrigerator. The milk in Jar 3 should also smell normal because the heating process should have killed most, if not all, of the bacteria. (**Note:** If you opened the heated jar after the first day, it is possible that bacteria floating in the air could have entered the jar and then the milk might have spoiled.)

Without bacteria, the milk cannot turn sour. Today, some milk companies, notably Parmalat™, use a heating process that destroys enough bacteria so that a sealed container of milk will stay fresh for several months without refrigeration.

Do not drink the milk after the experiment is over. Throw all three jars away or pour the milk down the drain.

THE COOLING CYCLE

When a gas expands, it generally gets cooler. When it contracts or condenses it gets warmer. We have all used this principle at one time or another.

If our food is too hot, what do we do? We blow on it.

Why does this cool the food down? When we blow out, the air pressure inside our mouth is greater than the pressure outside our mouth. We change the pressure by controlling our breathing apparatus (diaphragm and lungs), as well as the different parts of our mouth (lips and tongue). When we blow out we usually purse our lips, and as the air from our mouth escapes from our lips, it starts to expand. As it expands it gets cooler.

When that cool air comes in contact with the hot food, it absorbs some of the heat and takes it away from the food. On

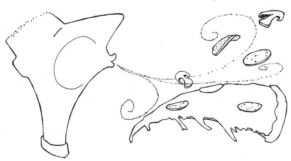

top of this, there is an effect like the "wind-chill factor" weather reporters are always talking about during the winter: Moving air removes more heat energy than air that is standing still.

It is also the expansion of matter that cools us down when we sweat. As we sweat, the drops of moisture absorb heat from our skin. As the sweat gets warmer, it expands. With the proper temperature and *humidity*, the sweat evaporates, carrying heat with it. That is how sweating helps us cool down. Sometimes, the air is so humid that it doesn't allow the sweat to turn into a gas. When that happens we get sweaty, sticky, wet, and feel yucky.

Sweating serves a number of purposes. One of them is to rid the body of waste products, such as excess salt and toxic byproducts of the body's metabolic functions. More important, sweating helps regulate the body's temperature. If the body cannot cool itself down through sweating, it can overheat, causing many medical problems, including heatstroke. This can happen in very damp, moist places like a tropical rain forest or even in cities with high humidity such as St. Louis, Missouri, or Chicago, Illinois.

At other times, the weather can be so hot and dry (the opposite of humid) that sweat evaporates as soon as it comes through your pores. It helps keep you cool, but you don't even know you've been sweating. This can happen in a hot desert or even in a city such as Phoenix, Arizona, during the summer months and it can be as dangerous as very humid weather.

The danger is that if you don't take in enough water by drinking, you may dehydrate, overheat, and get heatstroke. This can sneak up on anyone whose body runs out of water before the person feels thirsty. It has happened to me while I was exploring archaeological sites in the Egyptian desert.

While walking from one site to another, I remarked to my wife that my back was aching. She realized that my kidneys were acting up due to a lack of water in my system. After drinking lots of water, I started to feel better. For the rest of the trip I drank water every half hour whether I was thirsty or not.

HOW DOES A REFRIGERATOR KEEP THINGS COLD?

A refrigerator is basically an insulated box with a built-in heat pump. A heat pump moves heat from one place to another. In the case of a refrigerator, a heat pump moves heat from the inside of the insulated box to the outside of the box. In the case of an air conditioner, a heat pump moves the heat from the inside of a building or car to the outside. Sometimes, heat pumps are used as heaters. They can take heat from the outside air and transfer it into a house. This type of heater is used in warm climates.

When you place food in the refrigerator, the heat from the food is transferred to the air and inside walls of the refrigerator by radiation, convection, and conduction. This heat is then transferred to a coolant that circulates throughout the refrigerator's walls. A compressor compresses and liquefies the gas, which raises its temperature, and it then leaves the refrigerator "box" and enters some coils—usually on the back of the refrigerator's exterior, where they can't be seen. The heat from the coolant in these coils is then absorbed by the air in the kitchen, until the coolant is the same temperature as the air.

Finally, the liquid coolant returns to the tubes inside the refrigerator, and is allowed to expand again into a now much cooler gas. Heat from the food and the air in the fridge is again transferred to the coolant. It travels to the compressor where it is once more liquefied and moves on again to the rear of the refrigerator, where it again gives up the heat it has gained. This process repeats itself until the refrigerator is shut off.

compressor

coils
(on outside back wall
of refrigerator)

CAN A REFRIGERATOR COOL A HOUSE?

You might think you could cool your entire home by leaving the refrigerator door open, but it won't work. A refrigerator removes heat from the insulated portion of the box, where you store the food, and transfers that heat into the area outside the box, usually through the coils on the outside back wall.

So, while the inside of the refrigerator cools off, the outside heats up. As a matter of fact, not only does the heat from the insulated part of the box end up in the room, but so does the heat made by the mechanical action of the compressor. If you allowed the refrigerator to work with the door open for any length of time, the air in the room would become warmer, not cooler.

CHAPTER SEVEN

More About Refrigerators

Long before electric refrigerators were developed, people kept food in iceboxes—an insulated wooden box with doors on the front. The iceman pulled up on his horse-drawn cart and usually yelled out "ICE! ICE FOR SALE!" In many households, a child would be sent after the iceman to let him know that the family wanted to buy some. The iceman then used his "ice pick" to carve a piece of ice that was just the right size to fit the icebox. He carried the ice into the kitchen, opened the top door of the icebox, and put the ice block into a metal tray.

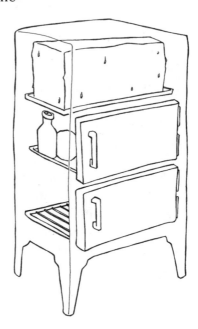

The ice cooled the air in the box. The cool air, being heavier than warm air, flowed downward and filled the lower portion of the icebox. But, as soon as one of the lower doors was opened, the cool air flowed out and warm air rushed in. The less you opened the icebox, the longer the ice lasted.

The latches on iceboxes were sturdy. Once they were closed, they stayed closed. They were designed so that they could not open accidentally. When electric refrigerators were introduced, the same type of thinking went into the design of their latches. Originally, the latches were made to be just as sturdy as those on the old iceboxes, and they could only be opened from the outside.

When electric refrigerators got old and were thrown out, they were frequently left on the sidewalk for the garbage collector, or sometimes, long before we learned about ecology, they were just dumped in empty lots. Little kids liked to play in these discarded refrigerators. Sometimes the door of one would slam shut and a child would be trapped inside. Manufacturers were pressured by consumer groups and the government to provide a safety catch that could be opened from the inside as well as from the outside. After trying out a number of designs, they decided that a magnetic door seal would be the most effective way to prevent anyone from being trapped inside.

OPENING THE REFRIGERATOR DOOR

When you open your refrigerator, the cold air inside, which is denser than the air in the kitchen, pours out and flows onto the floor of the kitchen while warm air from the kitchen flows into the refrigerator. This is a form of convection.

When the door of the refrigerator is closed, the warm air that has flowed inside starts to cool down. As the air starts to cool, it condenses and contracts, so the air pressure inside the refrigerator becomes somewhat lower than the air pressure outside. As a result of this cooling and contracting, the force of the air pushing on the outside walls of the refrigerator is now greater than the force of the air pushing against the inside walls of the refrigerator. This firmer push (after all, a force is a push or a pull) on the outside can make it difficult for you to open the door.

EXPERIMENT 9

Materials

A kitchen refrigerator with a magnetic latch
A fisherman's scale, capable of measuring forces of up to 50
 pounds (23 kg)
Strong string or cord
A warm day

Procedure

1. Tie a piece of string around the refrigerator's door han-
    dle and attach the fisherman's scale to the other end.

2. Tie a second piece of string to the other end of the
    scale.
3. Pull on the string—exerting a slow, steady force—until
    the refrigerator door opens. Note the reading on the
    scale when the door opens.
4. Close the door and open it again at once, noting the
    force needed this time.

5. Close the door and wait for 15 minutes. Then re-open the door, and again note how much force you exerted.
6. Try this a number of times. Each time, wait longer before you open the door.

Results

The readings on the fisherman's scale should give you a good idea of how much the cooling of the air in the refrigerator reduces the pressure inside, making it harder to open the door.

OBSERVATION 5

Whenever you open a refrigerator door, a lightbulb above the top shelf illuminates the inside, so you can see the food. Have you ever wondered whether that light stays on all the time? It doesn't.

Just to be sure, you might want to look for the switch. Where is it? Look at the areas where the refrigerator door contacts the frame around it. When you find it, you can turn the light in the refrigerator on and off without closing the door.

YOU CAN'T REFRIGERATE EVERYTHING

If you were to keep a bottle or jar of spices in the refrigerator, you'd eventually run into a problem. If the *relative humidity* in the kitchen was high, water vapor in the air would enter the jar when you opened it.

If that jar was then placed in the refrigerator, the air inside the jar would cool down. Since cool air cannot hold as much moisture as warm air, some of the moisture would condense as water droplets. Basically, a miniature rain shower would occur inside the jar. The spices would absorb the water drops, and start to spoil. Frost forms in the freezer compartment in a similar way.

A FROSTY FREEZER

Frost buildup sometimes occurs in refrigerator freezers because of moisture in the air. When the door of the freezer compartment is opened, warm, moist air enters the freezer. When the door is shut, the air cools down and the water in the air condenses as drops of water. These water drops often form on the metal parts of the freezer. As the water continues to cool down it eventually falls below 32°F (0°C)—the freezing point of water —and turns to ice. Water will also change from a gaseous state (water vapor) to a solid state (ice), bypassing the liquid state. When this happens, the frost in a freezer takes on a "feathery" appearance.

CHAPTER EIGHT

Air Pressure

The refrigerator can be a good laboratory. Have you ever noticed what happens when you put an almost-empty bottle of soda back in the refrigerator? A few hours later, the bottle may be a little crumpled because of a difference in air pressure—the same principle that makes a vacuum cleaner work. You can do the following experiments at home to investigate it.

EXPERIMENT 10

Materials
Three clean, empty plastic soda bottles with caps
Masking tape
A marking pen

Procedure
1. Using the marking pen and masking tape, label the bottles 1, 2, and 3.
2. Fill Bottle 1 with tap water. Bottles 2 and 3 will remain empty.
3. Screw the caps tightly onto all three bottles, making each bottle watertight and airtight.
4. Place Bottle 1 and Bottle 2 in the freezer compartment of your refrigerator. Leave Bottle 3 on a nearby counter or on top of the refrigerator. This bottle will be the experimental control.

5. After 30 minutes, open the freezer and take out Bottle 1 and Bottle 2. Compare these bottles to Bottle 3.

Results

Bottle 1 should look pretty much the same as before you put it in the freezer. The water will not freeze in such a short period of time. Bottle 3 should also look the same. But, the sides of Bottle 2 should have collapsed, so that the bottle looks squashed.

As the air trapped inside the bottle cooled off (gave up heat), the air started to contract because the lack of heat slowed down the movement of the air moleules. The air pressure within the bottle decreased until it was considerably less than the air pressure outside the bottle. Then when the air pressure outside the bottle pushed against the bottle, the air pressure inside was not great enough to push back. As a result, Bottle 2 collapsed.

EXPERIMENT 11

Materials
Three clean, empty plastic soda bottles with screw-on caps
A marking pen
Masking tape
A pitcher of water that has been chilled in the refrigerator
Hot water from the tap

Procedure
1. Using the marking pen and masking tape, label the bottles 1, 2, and 3.
2. Fill Bottle 1 with hot water from the tap and Bottle 2 with the cold, refrigerated water.
3. Pour all the water out of Bottle 1 and quickly screw the cap on tightly.
4. Pour all the water out of Bottle 2 and quickly screw the cap on tightly.
5. Screw the cap tightly on Bottle 3, which will be the experimental control.

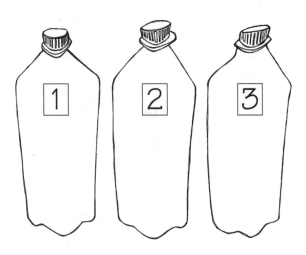

6. Place all three bottles on a table at least 12 inches (30 cm) away from each other and watch them for 10 minutes.

Results

Bottle 2 and Bottle 3 should not have changed, but Bottle 1 should have collapsed. When you poured the hot water out, the bottle and the air that entered it were warmer than room temperature. Because you capped the bottle tightly, more air from the room could not enter the bottle. When the air in Bottle 1 cooled down, it contracted. As it contracted, the air pressure dropped—there was less air pressure inside the bottle than outside. So the bottle was squeezed by the greater air pressure outside.

EXPERIMENT 12

Materials

A clean, plastic soda bottle with a screw-on cap
A *glass* medicine dropper
A large kitchen pot, about 6 inches (15 cm) deep
A pitcher of water
A nasty, stormy day

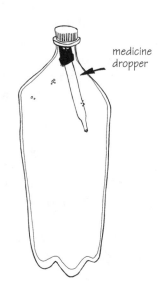

medicine dropper

Procedure

1. Fill the medicine dropper and pot with cold water. Put the dropper—bulb up—into the pot. The dropper should sink to the bottom.
2. Remove the dropper from the pot and remove water from the dropper—one drop at a time—until the dropper floats. Empty the pot and put it away.
3. Fill the soda bottle to the top with cold water, then put the dropper into the bottle. The dropper will

remain at the top of the water. Screw the bottle cap on tightly.

4. Examine the bottle each day for several days.

Results

After the storm passes and the weather gets nice and sunny, the dropper should sink to the bottom of the bottle. Why do you think this happened?

What you have made with the soda bottle and the medicine dropper is a type of barometer, a device that measures air pressure. In fact this type of barometer is also a toy, called a Cartesian Diver. It is named after French scientist René Descartes (1596–1650).

Air pressure is lower on stormy days than it is on sunny days. As the storm passes and the weather changes for the better, air pressure increases and squeezes the bottle. When the sides of the bottle are squeezed, pressure within the bottle is increased. Air, a gas, is easily compressed. Water, a liquid, is difficult to compress. That is why, when the pressure increases, the air in the medicine dropper's glass tube is compressed and forced up into the rubber bulb, and water from the bottle presses in and fills the lower part of the dropper.

As water is forced into the dropper the total density of the air-water combination in it increases. The amount of air in the dropper is the same, but additional water has been forced in, too. This increase in density makes the dropper less *buoyant*, and it sinks to the bottom of the bottle.

To use your barometer as a toy, just rest the bottle on a tabletop and squeeze it. As the pressure inside increases, you will see the dropper sink to the bottom. When you stop squeezing the bottle, the pressure inside decreases, the air inside expands again, and a small amount of water is forced out of the dropper. As a result, the density inside the dropper decreases and it floats back to the top of the bottle.

VACUUM CLEANERS

Most people think that vacuum cleaners clean things up by sucking in air. The way that vacuum cleaners actually work might seem a little strange—they make a partial *vacuum*, which is how they got their name. Look at the picture of the vacuum cleaner. There's a tube at one end, a body consisting of a motor, a fan, and a filter bag in the middle, and an exhaust vent at the other end.

When you start the vacuum cleaner, the motor begins to turn the fan. The fan pushes air out of the exhaust vent. Because the air is pushed out of the exhaust vent, an area of low pressure is formed in front of the fan. Since air tends to move from high pressure areas to low pressure areas, the air in the filter bag moves toward the fan. In turn, the air in the body of the vacuum cleaner moves toward the filter bag, and so does the air in the tube. This forms an area of low pressure in the

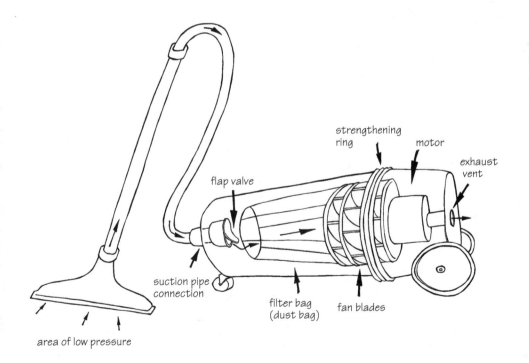

strengthening ring

motor

exhaust vent

flap valve

suction pipe connection

filter bag (dust bag)

fan blades

area of low pressure

tube, and air in the room moves toward it, dragging dust and dirt along with it into the tube, and then into the filter bag.

Eventually, the bag gets filled with debris and air can't pass through its walls. At that point the bag must be changed. If the bag is not changed, the vacuum cleaner will not pick up any more dirt.

In addition to carying dirt into the bag, the air rushing through the body of the cleaner cools down the motor. If there is not enough air moving over the motor to cool it down, the motor will burn out.

Review of Basic Scientific Principles

THE THREE STATES OF MATTER

All matter on Earth exists in one of three states—*solid, liquid,* or *gas.* Under the right conditions, a solid can be changed into a liquid, and then into a gas. For example when ice, a solid, is heated it can turn into water. When water is heated it can turn into vapor, a gas.

A solid has both a definite shape and a definite volume. We can change the volume of a solid by heating or cooling it. Examples of solids in your home include the wood that makes up a door, the glass in a window, the iron in a horseshoe, and so forth.

A liquid has a definite volume, but no definite shape because the molecules of a liquid slip and slide around each other very easily. One way that we can lock the molecules together is by cooling the liquid down. If we cool it down enough it becomes a solid, such as ice. Some examples of liquids in your home are: water, soda, coffee, shampoo, and cooking oil.

At a constant temperature a gas has neither a definite volume nor a definite shape. That means we can force the gas into almost any shape that we want. It also means that we can change the volume of the gas—the amount of space that it takes up. There are two ways to do this. We can heat it or cool it, or we can compress or decompress it. Examples of gases in the home are the air we breathe, the air in a basketball or football, the bubbles in a bottle of soda, and the "stuff" that makes sprays like air freshener or hair spray.

HOW AIR PRESSURE INFLUENCES BOILING POINT

At sea level, standard air pressure is 14.7 pounds per square inch (1 kg/cm^2). At this altitude, liquid water's boiling point—the point where it becomes a gas—is 212°F (100°C). If the temperature of water is less than 212°F it stays liquid. If it is any more than 212°F, it becomes a gas.

As the liquid turns into a gas, it becomes much less dense. It then rises above the water, taking heat energy with it—which keeps the remaining water at 212°F.

If we change the air pressure on the water, we can change the boiling point. For instance, in Denver, Colorado, which is about 1 mile (1.6 km) above sea level, air pressure is less than 14.7 pounds per square inch (1 kg/cm^2). In the lower air pressure, water becomes a gas at a lower temperature and so water boils at approximately 190°F (88°C).

If, on the other hand, we use a pressure cooker at sea level, we can raise the pressure on the water to more than 14.7 pounds per square inch (1 kg/cm^2). Then the boiling point of water can be increased to approximately 225° to 240°F (107° to 116°C), depending on the amount of added pressure.

SIMPLE MACHINES

A number of simple machines were mentioned briefly throughout this book. The information below will give you a little more information about how each of them works.

The Lever

A *lever* is a bar that turns about a pivot point and is used to transfer force. A lever's pivot point is called the *fulcrum*. We usually use a lever to increase the force we put into an action. Whenever a lever is used, a certain tradeoff is involved. In order for the input force to be multiplied, the object must be moved over a greater distance.

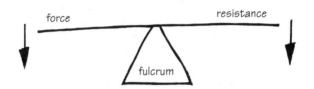

There are three types of levers. A first-class lever has a force at one end, the resistance or load on the other end, and a fulcrum in the center. When you turn the handle of a faucet, you supply the input force to the outer portion of the handle, the center of the handle acts as the pivotal point, and the screw inside the faucet offers resistance. Other first-class levers include wrenches, pliers, and scissors.

Second- and third-class levers are similar to a first-class lever, except that the positions of the fulcrum, input force, and resistance are different. Garlic presses, nutcrackers, and egg slicers are examples of second-class levers, while ice tongs and a hammer used to drive a nail are examples of third-class levers.

The Inclined Plane

An *inclined plane* is a plane surface that is set at an angle. A plank going from the ground to the back of a truck is an inclined plane. It is easier to push a heavy object up a ramp than it is to lift it the same distance, even though the force must be exerted over a greater distance. Examples of inclined planes include the cutting edge of a hatchet or axe and the point of a nail.

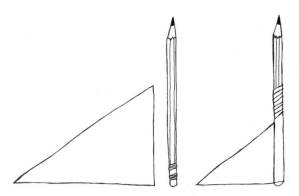

Screws and bolts are special types of inclined plane. To see this better, wrap a triangular piece of paper—an inclined plane—around a pencil, as shown in the illustration above. As the pencil is wrapped around the pencil, you will see that it begins to look like the threads of a screw.

As you twist a screw into a piece of wood, it travels a greater distance than if you had just pushed it straight in. But overall, less force is required to force the screw into the wood by screwing it than by pushing it.

The Wheel and Axle

A wheel is a circular object with a center attached to a rod or bar called an axle. Together the wheel and axle act as a single tool that helps decrease friction and allows the input force to be multiplied. A wheel and axle can be thought of as a circular lever.

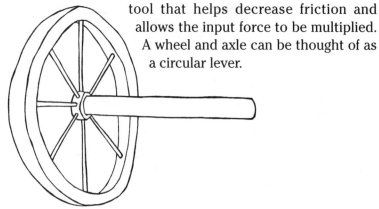

The Pulley

A pulley is a special type of wheel. The axle of the wheel is attached to a device called a bale and the outer circumference of the wheel is grooved to hold a rope or cable in place. A simple pulley can be used to change the direction of applied force. A compound pulley or block and tackle can change the direction of the applied force as well as the force's magnitude. As is true of the inclined plane and the lever, the distance the input force must travel is increased when this simple tool is used.

Glossary

absorb to soak up a liquid or gas as a sponge sops up water.

atom the smallest part of an element that can exist and still keep the properties of that element.

buoyancy the upward force on an object in a fluid, which appears to counteract gravity. Examples are a wooden spoon floating in a sink full of water and a helium balloon floating up in the air.

centrifugal force the force that an object moving along a circular path exerts outwardly. It is directed against the body that is constraining the object to its circular path.

cohesion an attraction between molecules that holds them close together.

conduction the transmission of heat energy from a warmer object to a cooler object.

conductor a material that can transmit energy, particularly heat.

control an untested sample providing a standard against which the tested experimental samples can be compared.

convection the transfer of heat by the movement of the fluid.

electromagnetic spectrum the total range of electromagnetic radiation, ranging from the longest wavelength radio waves to the shortest gamma rays. The electromagnetic spectrum also includes ultraviolet and infrared energy, visible light, X rays, and microwaves.

evaporation the process by which a liquid is transformed to a gas.

first-class lever a lever with the force on one end, the resistance (or load) on the other end, and a fulcrum in the center.

force a push or a pull

friction the force that resists the motion of one object that is in contact with another object. This force causes heat to be produced when the two objects are moved against each other.

fulcrum the point around which a lever pivots.

gas one of the three states of matter. Matter that has neither a definite shape nor a definite volume.

gravity a force that pulls objects toward Earth's surface.

humidity the amount of moisture (water vapor) in the air.

inclined plane a plane surface that is set at an angle.

insulator a material that does not transmit heat (or another form of energy) well.

intra-molecular a force acting within a molecule.

lever a bar that turns about a pivot point and is used to transfer force.

liquid one of the three states of matter. Matter that has a definite volume but no definite shape.

matter physical substance or stuff. Everything in the universe that isn't empty space or energy.

molecule one of the basic units forming a chemical compound. The smallest molecules contain one atom, but most molecules are composed of more than one atom. The atoms making up a molecule can be of the same element or of different elements. Water (H_2O) is made up of the elements hydrogen and oxygen, two atoms of hydrogen (H) to one atom of oxygen (O). Table salt (NaCl) is one atom of sodium (Na) combined with one atom of chlorine (Cl). An oxygen molecule is made up of two atoms and is written as O_2. Ozone (O_3) is made of three atoms of oxygen.

plunger a device used to unclog pipes.

pressure a force acting on a surface. Air pressure is measured in pounds per square inch (lb./in^2) or grams per square centimeter (g/cm^2).

radiation the transfer of heat energy by waves (such as light waves).

relative humidity the relationship between the amount of water vapor in the air and the maximum amount that it can hold at that temperature. This is usually expressed as a percentage. A high relative humidity such as 80 percent or more is generally uncomfortable (too wet), as is a low relative humidity of 30 percent or less (too dry).

rotational inertia see **centrifugal force**.

solid one of the three states of matter. Matter that has both a definite shape and a definite volume.

surface tension a property of the surface of a liquid that makes the surface pull together to take up the smallest possible area. It is caused by the attraction of molecules in the liquid.

vacuum an area that has a low gas pressure. A perfect vacuum would have no molecules of gas within it at all. At sea level, an air pressure of less than 14.7 pounds per square inch (1 kg/cm^3) results in a partial vacuum.

Resources

BOOKS

Epstein, Lewis Carroll. *Thinking Physics*. San Francisco: Insight Press, 1978.

Gonnick, Larry, *The Cartoon Guide To Physics*, New York: Harper Collins, 1990.

Grolier Multimedia Encyclopedia, release 6. Danbury, CT: Grolier Electronic Publishing, 1993.

Macaulay, David. *The Way Things Work*. Boston: Houghton Mifflin, 1988.

McGraw-Hill Concise Encyclopedia of Science and Technology. New York: McGraw-Hill, 1984.

Walker, Jearl. *The Flying Circus of Physics*. New York: John Wiley & Sons, 1977

INTERNET SITES

Due to the changeable nature of the Internet, sites appear and disappear very quickly. Those listed below offered useful information at the time of publication.

Dr. Internet is a guide to science experiments and science sites on the Internet.
http://ipl.sils.umich.edu/youth/DrInternet/

Helping Your Child Learn Science is an online book full of activities and experiments that can be done at home.
http://www.ed.gov/pubs/parents/Science/index.html

The Mad Scientist Network is a network of more than 200 scientists around the world who will try to answer any question you come up with.
http://medinfo.wustl.edu/~ysp/MSN/

MicroScapes Gallery features microscopic photos of everyday objects.
http://www.att.com/
microscapes/microscapes.html

The Miami Museum of Science has a site that lists chemistry experiments and has information about all kinds of science exhibits.
http://www.miamisci.org/ph/

The Super Science Site provides help with science experiments, and has tips for experiments with everyday things.
http://www.superscience.com/home.html

If you visit the YES Mag: Canada's Online Science Magazine site you can find out about science news, projects, and more.
http://www.islandnet.com/~yesmag/homepage.html

Index